Pieces of Mind

Poetry of sorts

FSC
www.fsc.org
MIX
Papir fra
ansvarlige kilder
Paper from
responsible sources
FSC® C105338

Publisher: BoD – Hellerup, Denmark
Printing: BoD – Norderstedt, Germany

ISBN: 978-87-4302-837-6

How do you do

She asked
'What do you do with your life?'
And she told me
about the sins of man,
of eternal damnation,
of doomsday imminent.
And I said,
'I make love'.

The key

Find the key
to the door of wonders.
Never forget
to roam the stars.
Let your heart
rejoice
to sunlight on leaves,
raindrops and laughter.
Lead your steps
to east of the sun
and west of the moon.
Let the door stand ajar.

Voyage

A tiny blue dot
thundering through eternity
teeming with life
for the briefest of moments.
Precious and fragile
silicon consciousness
travelling hopefully
across the multiverse.

Childhood

The school yard is empty.
Well, almost empty.
There is the wind
and the gentle rustling
of torn candy wrapping;
even the faint echoes
of children's voices
have all gone.
She sits there
in her little blue car,
the teacher's daughter
drinking in the silence
scanning the yard
for the flickering images
from her imagination,
waiting for them
to populate her world
with make believe people.

And she treads on,
driving her car
into private realms
unseen by others.

5

Summer in Norrland

Sometimes you see
the pale light
before dawn
through steamed windows
and blurry eyes.
Watch the tall pines
and the road
– a dirt track
for elks or goblins
or maybe bears.
You can't sleep;
there's no dark
no bedtime
just this pale light
between day and day
when the elves dance.

Hope for a new Sutra

The old Sutra said
No colour, no sound,
no thought, no form.
Will the day come
for us to say
No pain, no fear,
no anguish, no war?

Musse Morning

Silence is hovering
over the fields
gently stirred
by the rising sun.
The sparrows settle
on my garden table;
morning has broken.

Dreaming

I daydream a lot.
Swirls of imagination
ties into a noose
to capture tomorrow.
I cling to it –
drag myself along.
And suddenly
I have arrived.

Hit or miss

Inspiration
sleets through the universe,
photons of creativity
hit random minds.
Sometimes
they explode,
unfold,
become.

Angels

Angels
beings of light
figments of imagination
avengers
and saviours.
Are they who
or what?

In memoriam

I didn't know
a home
could be this silent.
I never knew
all those little noises
now confusing me.
I hear your footsteps
the front door
light switches
the car coming into the driveway.
All the time
I listen
for any sound
that might be you
although I know
it cannot be.

There is nothing now
but the wind
and the creaks.
Nothing left
but the silence
of being alone.

Play

They sat on the floor,
the old man
and the child.
Look, grandpa
this is the money
and this is the groceries,
the child pointed.
And the old man smiled
and changed his voice –
Good morning madam
I would like to buy...
The little girl
beamed happily at him,
he really knew
how to play.

Relationship

There was...
and then she said...
and then he said...
and afterwards she heard...
and someone told him...
and then...
It started all over again...
and so he said...
and...

Family

My mother said
'tell him not to'.
My sister said
'don't let him'.
But I say
'how could I?
How could I ever ask of him
to cripple himself
to be a lesser man?'

Anticipation

Eagerly awaiting
the arrival
of the master.
Learning is imminent,
hovering in the air
like mosquitoes
waiting to sting.

Café

Faces
like random dots;
separate minds
in little patches
of loneliness.
Eyes scanning
for movements
of the recognisable,
waiting for no one
hoping for anyone
to come.

Anger

Got this thing with stones you know.
Gotta kick them.
Imagine they're my boss or
something.
Or my goddamn brother.
It's a Freud thing they say.
What's a Freud?

Do you see me

When you look at me
what do you see?
Do you see
the little girl
with the glasses,
the agile dancer
in the see-through dress
or the tired mother
holding her child?
What do you read
in the lines of my face?
My anger,
my age
or the wear and tear
of smiling?

When you look in my eyes
do you see my worries,
my wishes,
my love,
or do you see
a reflection of you?

January

The snow is melting
like my own hopes.
I feel as barren
as the brown fields outside
filled with little puddles of despair.
Is spring coming?
Is joy?
Now everything
just seeps silently into the ground.
Greyness of sky
mingle with greyness of mind.
The pretty soft cover has all gone
leaving everything exposed.

Mail

Got this mail thing.
Fast stuff.
You can even send pictures.
It's like real easy.
You can send
to a hundred friends at a time.
Now I just need some friends.

This land

There's this land
of hope and glory.
Who's land?
Who's glory?
Who's hope?

Moving house

The music's there and Nelly talking
and the stove's on and it's all
fragmenting into split second colours
and my arm hurts and why's the
trolley blue, just tell me, and mind the
steps.
I didn't like this place but the carpet's
soft so leave the shoes at the door
and the brain on the mantelpiece, you
won't need neither as long as the
coffee's hot, but that's just what Colin
said since we painted the chairs, yeah,
and watch out for the dog, you might
step on it.

Leaving home

They said to me
you cannot
you shouldn't
I won't have it
it's not good for you
think of the others
what would your father say
don't you realize
you call this gratitude?
And all I could say
was
'goodbye'.

Joy

Listen
to the fragrance
of roses.
Touch
the echo
of a butterfly's wing.
Taste
the brilliance
of sunlight.
Embrace
the flavour
of love.

Memories

Memories
in the gumbo
of mind
stirring
little bubbles
popping
on the surface.
Feel
the heat
touch
the steam
smell
the wafting scents
of yesterday.

The Yous

Have you ever
met yourself?
The child,
the graduate,
the first you
who was really you?
Can you reach out
to a future you
hold hands
with yourself
across the years?
Do you acknowledge
the changes,
appreciate
the journey,
embrace
the coming of age?

Geek

So they call you a geek
make fun of your hair
point at your clothes
shout abuse at you.
But they don't know
that you can take it off
leave it behind
be whoever you want,
whereas they
however much they try
cannot change,
cannot escape
the confines of normality.

Dance

The body awakens,
silent circuits connect.
My blood sings with music,
fizzing and laughing.
I flex my muscles
cautious like a bird
out of a cage.
I dance again
lose myself –
dissolve into motion.

Worlds

Show me your world
and I'll show you mine.
Let's forget about consensus
leave out the compromise
just be who we are.
Your world is other
so mine is to you,
no better no worse
not right nor wrong
only not the same.
Let's keep our worlds
separate and together
sharing but different.

For Thomas

Life can be left
leaving treasured memories
never to fade.
Life can go on
weaving different patterns
present and past.
Life can be shared
with moments of happiness
carried in love.

Love song

Meet me
at the mound of Áine.
Touch me
till I spread my wings.
I'll reach you
at the mound of Áine,
touch you
till your body sings.

Join me
at the mound of Áine.
Love me,
till your soul meets mine.
I'll hold you
at the mound of Áine
love you,
till my heart meets thine.

Lies

I see a lie
flickering in your eyes;
I hear its song
echo in your speech,
watch it subtly change
the way you walk.
It's been weeks now
and it's getting stronger.
I only wish
I dared ask
dare rip it's veil
and look it in the face
but I do not.
I shy away,
fearful that it might hurt
even more than half hidden;
fearful that you might leave me
with only the lie
to remember you by.

Echoes

Do you Listen
to the echoes in your mind?
The distant roar of the waves –
the faint noise of scales on sand?
Do you hear
the earth move?
Feel the vibrations in your body
of the thundering herds?
Can you ride your thoughts
by spreading your wings,
surfing the thermals of the sun?
Have you tried
to listen with your nose
see with your feet
taste the air
as you once did?

When you close your hand
Does it grip the axe
or hold the child?
Can you raise your arm,
poised for the perfect throw
or bend your ankle just right
for the menuet?

It is all there
like echoes engraved.
Memories
from when the first stars were born.
The endless darkness
an eternity of loneliness
and then –
the many, the travelling, and love.

To know

You're indecisive you say.
Know yourself, I say.
True knowledge
give all the answers
before the question even arises.
If you know your heart
it's only to follow
and the yeas and nays of life
are readily there.
So be silent,
really be silent,
take time
to listen
to commune with your self.

Consolation

When you are sad
you find Prozac in ice cream
and opium in chocolate.
You seek friendship in cream cheese
and love in a cracker.
Like a desperate moth
you move between lights
of tv's and fridges,
and your mind calms a bit
sedated in sugars,
building walls of protection
to keep out the hurt.

Leaving

I just found your sock.
You know the red one?
The one we thought the dog ate.
It was behind the sofa.
Imagine – all these years...
Did you take the other one with you
when you left?

Row

Words hovering
over the table
fusing together,
growing tiny edges.
Nothing to be seen –
just pinpoints of radiation
emitting anger,
building a haze,
distorting everything.

Recycling

Treasure your body.
Behold the billions of atoms
from the dawn of time.
Once part of great stars
long since faded;
once sizzling in a pool
of boiling hot acid.
Once breathed by people
afraid of mammoths.
Think of yourself
as one of the star-people –
the ancestors of old.
Feel at one with nature
because you are truly One.

Every bit of you
eternal like the universe
is just on loan
for the briefest of moments
carrying on
till the end of the world.

Summer Night

I put on the night,
rest my head against the wind.
I bed down the geese,
bid the sparrows goodnight
and welcome the nightingale.
I perfume myself
with the scent of thyme and roses,
take a shower in moonlight
and borrow the wings of a moth.

Universe

There was emergence –
mists of matter
Stars were born and died.
And now
yet more stars,
planets
and us –
all stardust reborn.
Once along the way
consciousness happened
But when?
Or was it there
from the very beginning?
Or could it be
that consciousness
is all there is
and all
there ever was?

To Gabriela

There was this dark hall and rustling of
many and a funny man on a stage,
and then this roaring laughter
rose like Kundalini
conjuring up a feeling of commune
and faces became friends
and then words filled the space
between minds and ignited,
opening windows of understanding,
and thoughts leapt out of skulls
soaring the skies together,
twittering excitedly
not all listening but all sharing
and later, much later,
little red marks of friendship
recognized each other
and touched once again.

The sickbed

She was running the show
with the whip of bad conscience,
being weak and in bed
craving evermore nursing.
From the fragile smiles
ruled the fist of a tyrant
demanding submission
from kin and friend alike.
Only all this attention
ease not the suffering
the ultimate loneliness
of the despot of hearts.

The rose

You remind me of roses –
the white roses in my garden,
thin stemmed and fragile
with big, fragrant blossoms
too heavy to carry.

They endow my garden
with scents of faraway places,
white silken petals
gently turning pink.
The flowers droop
as the stems give in
to the mighty weight of beauty;
no crutches to hold them
no hand ups from the leaves.

What is the burden
that you carry
bringing echoes of faraway places
needing the crutches
of binges or booze
or maybe
just someone to listen?

Tattoo

Little pictures
painted in ink and pain,
claiming ownership
or devotion;
bragging tales
of travels or conquests.
Tokens of manhood
or maybe drunkenness?
Moments lasting forever,
memories chiselled in skin.
Do you treasure
or regret?

Prayer

Give me the courage
to fight injustice.
Give me the strength
to love without conditions.
Give me the urge
to know about the world.
Give me the wisdom
to understand people.
Give me the words
to heal wounded hearts.

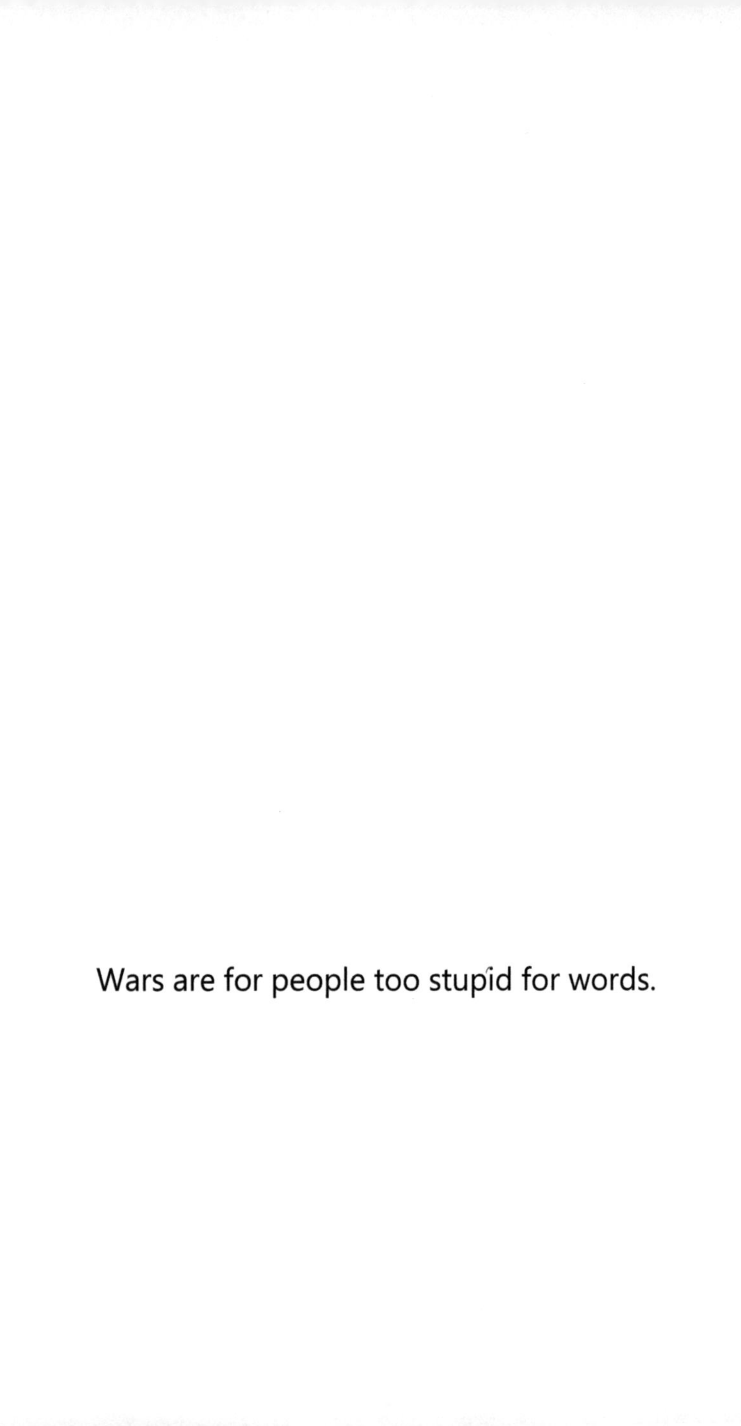

Wars are for people too stupid for words.

Don't change the curtains. Change your life!